Mary L Williams

God's Precious Boy
A Celebration of Spirituality

By Mary Lowe Williams
Photography by Connie Palen

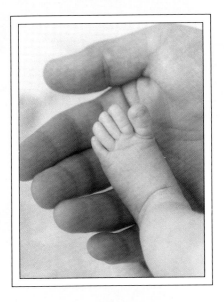

Health Communications, Inc.
Deerfield Beach, Florida

Warmth and Wonder for God's Precious Boy . . .

We invite you to share the warmth and wonder of Mary Lowe Williams' tender affirmations and Connie Palen's beautiful photographs which illuminate the uniqueness of every boy.

This lovely book powerfully, yet gently, affirms that all children are valuable, and deserve love and acceptance.

God's Precious Boy is a gift of love for children from 4 to 104. It touches the heart and soothes the spirit. Frequently read this book to your child or yourself and honor the preciousness in each of us.

We are delighted to share these spiritual affirmations with you, and hope they bring you many moments of serenity.

Health Communications, Inc.

©1992 Mary Lowe Williams
ISBN 1-55874-248-4

Publisher: Health Communications, Inc.
        3201 S.W. 15th Street
        Deerfield Beach, Florida 33442-8190

Dedicated to my son, Mark . . . .
May the innocence of a child lead you
to the wisdom of God.

*Am I really a precious
child of God?*

My mother says that God
loves me and that God
will *always* love me.

And God blesses me every day:

Thank you, God, for my dog.
Thank you for my space toys and
   telescope.
Thank you for all my books.
Thank you for swim team.
Thank you for my friends.
Thank you for Mom and Dad and
   my sister.
Thank you for Grandma and Papoo and
   Grandma L.
I am so lucky.
I love you, God.
I need you.

Thank you for loving me, God.

God is a mystery to me.

How did God make the moon and the
    stars, the sun and earth, the rainbows
    and sunsets?
Where is God?
Why can't I see God?
Does God get scared or sad?
Can God hear my prayers?

My father thinks God may
always be a mystery.
I *like* mysteries.

*Look at what God created
long ago.*

I enjoy learning about God's
many creations.

I can feel *God in my heart.*

I love knowing God
is always near.

I love to giggle and have fun.

Part of God's plan is for me to be happy.

All my feelings are important to God.

No matter how I feel, God accepts me just the way I am.

There are times when I am afraid to do things by myself.

Yet I feel safe because God looks after me.

*Sometimes everyone is
too busy for me.*

God puts many wonderful people
in my life. When someone
listens to me, I feel
important.

I try to do things to please my parents and friends but sometimes they are still unhappy.

My gift to others is *to be* myself, just as I am, the wonderful person God created. Even though I try, I may not be able to make someone else happy.

Sometimes I am angry and don't get along with others.

God wants me to say how I feel. Because I want others to listen to me, I will listen to them. We can ask each other for what we want and learn to give and take.

I wish I didn't make mistakes.

Making mistakes does not mean I am bad.
God knows making mistakes is the way
to learn. It means I need more time
and practice at something. I will
love myself, mistakes and all,
just as God loves me.

*I especially feel bad when
my mistakes hurt
someone else.*

Yet being angry with myself only
makes me feel worse. When
I say, "I'm sorry," and give
the person time to get
over being hurt, we
both feel better.

Everyone made fun of me when I cried at school today.

God gives me tears to
wash away my pain.
It's okay to cry.

I am glad that God made me a boy.

God also gives me the abilities
and freedom to become
whatever I desire.

When I am proud of
something I do, I
feel joyful and
excited.

God's spirit inside me says,
"You did it! Good job!"

My laughing, singing and dancing show God my thanks.

When I show how thankful I am, God is pleased.

I like to talk to God.

We are good friends.

*I can ask God for what
I need and want.*

I am learning to trust that God
knows best, and will give me
what I need when the
time is right.

*God wants me to
love myself.*

Loving myself feels good and
makes it easier to love
and accept others.

*I feel calm and
peaceful.*

Thank you, God, for your
presence in my life.

Yes, I am a precious
child of God.

Always.

More Valuable Resources From Mary L. Williams

I AM PRECIOUS relaxation and affirmation audiotapes for adults and children.

Slides of *MY PRECIOUS CHILD, GOD'S PRECIOUS BOY* and *GOD'S PRECIOUS GIRL* for professional use.

Lectures and workshops on dysfunctional families and on spirituality.

Write to:
Mary L. Williams
LOVING MATTERS
Box 1524
Glenwood Springs, CO 81602